Black Sketchbooks

1 London
2 Edinburgh
3 Cambridge
4 Stratford on Avon
5 Bath and Wells
6 Canterbury

PUBLISHED BY
A. & C. BLACK · SOHO SQUARE · LONDON W.

CANTERBURY.

A SKETCH BOOK

BY WALTER M. KEESEY.

A · & · C · BLACK · LIMITED · LONDON · 1915

Drawings.

THE APPROACH.

South Choir Aisle and Pilgrims' Steps.

THE CATHEDRAL CLOSE

THE TOMB OF THE
BLACK PRINCE

CORNER OF THE CLOISTERS.

W. M. KEESEY

THE CATHEDRAL CLOSE
FROM THE EAST

W.M. KEESEY 1914.

THE CHAPEL OF
OUR LADY OF THE UNDERCROFT.

THE CATHEDRAL EAST END
FROM LADY WOOTTON'S GREEN

THE CRYPT
UNDER THE CHOIR

THE CATHEDRAL
FROM THE FIELDS.

MINT YARD.
KING'S SCHOOL

W. H. KERSEY 1914

THE WESTGATE · EVENING ·

- Mercery Lane -

OLD HOUSE CORNER OF
THE FRIARS.

W.M. KEESEY '14

QUEEN ELIZABETH'S CHAMBERS.

W.M. KEESEY. 1914

· ST. THOMAS' HOSPITAL ·

WALTER M KEESEY

· THE BUTTER MARKET ·

· THE MILL ·

The Dane John

Borough Corner

THE NORMAN STAIRCASE

First published in Great Britain in 1915
by A&C Black Publishers
36 Soho Square
London W1D 3QY
www.acblack.com

This edition published 2009

ISBN 978-14081-1124-6

A CIP record of this book is available from the British Library

Printed and bound in China